Houghton Mifflin

English

Shirley Haley-James   John Warren Stewig

Marcus T. Ballenger   June Grant Shane

Jacqueline L. Chaparro   C. Ann Terry

Nancy C. Millett

Houghton Mifflin Company   Boston

Atlanta   Dallas   Geneva, Illinois   Lawrenceville, New Jersey   Palo Alto   Toronto

Acknowledgments

The publisher has made every effort to locate each owner of the copyrighted material reprinted here. Any information enabling the publisher to rectify or credit any reference is welcome.

The Bear's Toothache by David McPhail. Copyright © 1972 by David McPhail. By permission of Little, Brown and Company in association with The Atlantic Monthly Press.

The Forgetful Bears by Lawrence Weinberg, illustrated by Paula Winter. Illustrations copyright © 1981 by Paula Winter. Reprinted by permission of Ticknor & Fields/Clarion Books, a Houghton Mifflin Company, and Scholastic, Inc.

"The Letter" from *Frog and Toad Are Friends* by Arnold Lobel. Copyright © 1970 by Arnold Lobel. Reprinted by permission of Harper & Row, Publishers, Inc., and William Heinemann Limited.

"Lost in the Museum," from *Lost in the Museum* by Miriam Cohen, illustrations by Lillian Hoban. Illustrations copyright © 1979 by Lillian Hoban. By permission of Greenwillow Books (A Division of William Morrow & Co.).

"Lunch for a Dinosaur," by Bobbi Katz from the poem "Company" in *Upside Down and Inside Out: Poems for All Your Pockets*, published by Franklin Watts, Inc. Copyright © 1973 by Bobbi Katz. Reprinted by permission of the author.

Mike Mulligan and His Steam Shovel by Virginia Lee Burton. Copyright 1939 and © 1967 by Virginia Lee Demetrios. Reprinted by permission of Houghton Mifflin Company.

"Move Over," from *Little Raccoon and Poems from the Woods* by Lilian Moore. Copyright © 1975 by Lilian Moore. Reprinted by permission of Marian Reiner for the author.

"The Owl," from *Zoo Doings* by Jack Prelutsky. Copyright © 1967, 1983 by Jack Prelutsky. By permission of Greenwillow Books (A Division of William Morrow & Company).

"The Pickety Fence," from *Every Time I Climb a Tree* by David McCord. Copyright 1952, © 1972 by David McCord. By permission of Little, Brown and Company, and George Harrap, Ltd.

Credits

Series design concept and cover design by Ligature, Inc.

Front cover and title page photograph: Animals Animals © 1988 Lee Lockwood

Back cover and page 192: Ralph Brunke

Illustrations

Virginia Lee Burton: 14, 15, 16
Laura Ferraro: 107
Lilian Hoban: 86
Meg Kelleher: (borders) 81, 82, 103, 104, 107, 108, 138, 167, 179
Susan Lexa: 17, 19–21, 37–39, 55, 56, 71, 73–76, 79, 80, 82, 94, 97, 99, 100, 138, 157, 158, 163, 167, 168, 171, 172, 187, 196–206, *Opposites Game, Naming Word Game*
Arnold Lobel: 108
Jane McCreary: 35, 36, 41–44, 47–52, 77, 78, 81, 93, 101, 102, 105–107, 109–111, 123, 124, 131, 132, 134, 136, 143, 144, 159–162, 176, 183, 184
David McPhail: 11, 12
Paul Sances: (borders) 82, 103, 104, 138, 172, 184
Carol Schwartz: 141, 142, 143–144 (borders)
Ann Schweninger: 85, 86 (border)
Lou Vaccaro: 13, 23–28, 31, 33, 34, 63–68, 72, 95, 96, 125–130, 133, 135, 137, 139, 145, 169, 170, 175, 177, 178, 180–182, 185, 193–195, *Rhyme Game, Number Word Game, Sentence Game, Describing Word Game*
Joe Veno: (borders) 18, 19, 23–28, 88, 112, 113, 137, 145–147, 190
Paula Winter: 188

Photographs

10 Daemmrich. 21 Michal Heron. 22 Peter Fronk/Click/Chicago. 30 Ulrike Welsch. 46 Kim Massie/Rainbow. 54 Allen Green/Photo Researchers Inc. 70 James H. Simon/The Picture Cube. 84 Daemmrich. 92 Elwin Williamson/The Picture Cube. 106 Cezus/Click/Chicago. 122 Daemmrich. 140 Jane Burton/Bruce Coleman Inc. 156 Bill Binzen. 166 (left) The Image Bank. 166 (right) Chuck Fishman/Woodfin Camp & Assoc. 174 Frank Siteman/The Picture Cube. 186 Jeff Reed/The Stock Shop.

Victoria Beller-Smith: 29, 32, 45, 53, 87, 89–91, 104, 118, 121, 152, 155, 166

Table of Contents

5

Student's Resource Book 192

Punchouts
Games
The Rhyme Game
The Color Game
The Number Word Game
The Opposites Game
The Sentence Game
The Naming Word Game
The Describing Word Game
Book Covers
My Book About Me
My Book of Favorites
My Story

9

Readiness
Listening and Speaking

LISTENING

1 | Listening for Details

 Listen and look.

The Bear's Toothache
by DAVID MCPHAIL

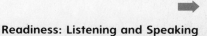

Children listen to a story, discuss illustrations, and recall details from the story.

 Remember and draw.

Children recall and draw an incident from the story.

LISTENING

2 | Listening for Rhyme

Listen and match.

Children listen to a poem and match pictures
illustrating rhyming words from the poem.

Readiness: Listening and Speaking

Name

3 | Listening for Sequence

Listen and look.

Mike Mulligan and His Steam Shovel
by VIRGINIA LEE BURTON

Readiness: Listening and Speaking

Children listen to a story and look at pictures showing the sequence of events.

Listening for Sequence continued

Children listen to a story and look at pictures
showing the sequence of events.

Listening for Sequence continued

Listen and color.

Readiness: Listening and Speaking

Children order pictures in the correct sequence.

SPEAKING

4 | Telling a Story

 Look and discuss.

1.

2.

3.

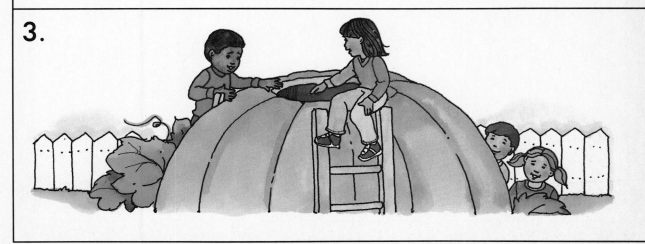

Children discuss pictures and tell a story to go along with them.

Readiness: Listening and Speaking

Telling a Story continued

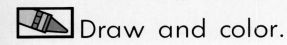Draw and color.

Readiness: Listening and Speaking

Children draw a picture illustrating an outcome of the story.

Name _____

SPEAKING

5 | Talking About Taking Turns

Discuss and mark.

Draw and color.

Children discuss, mark, and draw pictures.   **Readiness: Listening and Speaking**   19

SPEAKING

6 | Talking Without Words

Discuss and match.

1.

2.

3.

Readiness: Listening and Speaking

Children match situations and gestures.

SPEAKING

7 | Answering the Phone

Listen and mark.

Children mark pictures to answer questions about a telephone conversation.

Name _____

1 | A Picture of Me

My name is

_____

- -

_____ •

Children draw and discuss pictures of themselves.   **Readiness: My Book About Me**

Name _____

2 | Where I Live

Readiness: My Book About Me

Children draw and discuss pictures of their homes.

Name

3 | My Family

Children draw and share pictures of their families.

Readiness: My Book About Me

4 | My Best Friends

Readiness: My Book About Me   Children draw and discuss pictures of their best friends.

Name _____

5 | My School

The name of my school is

_____

- -

_____ •

Children draw and discuss pictures of their school.

6 | When I Grow Up

Readiness: My Book About Me

Children draw and discuss pictures of what they want to be when they grow up.

7 | Making My Book

Children make books of their finished drawings, using the covers provided at the back of the book.

Readiness: My Book About Me

Name _____

READINESS

LISTENING

1 | Following Directions

Listen and mark.

1.

2.

3.

Children listen to and follow one-step directions.

Readiness: Listening and Thinking 31

Copyright © 1988 by Houghton Mifflin Company. All rights reserved.

Following Directions continued

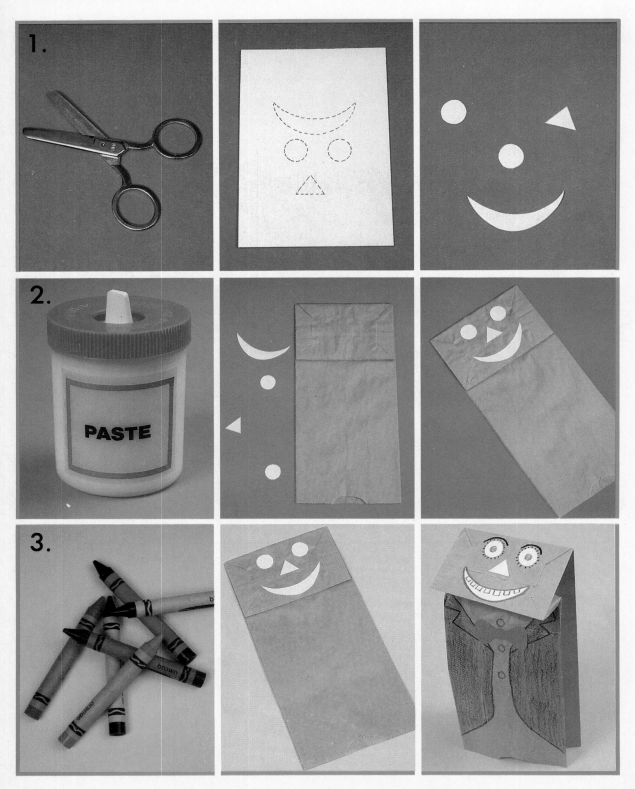

Listen and make.

1.

2.

3.

Readiness: Listening and Thinking

Children listen to and follow three-step directions.

Name _____

LISTENING

2 ‖ Colors

 Listen and color.

Children listen and color a picture according to teacher's directions.

Readiness: Listening and Thinking

Colors continued

 Look and color.

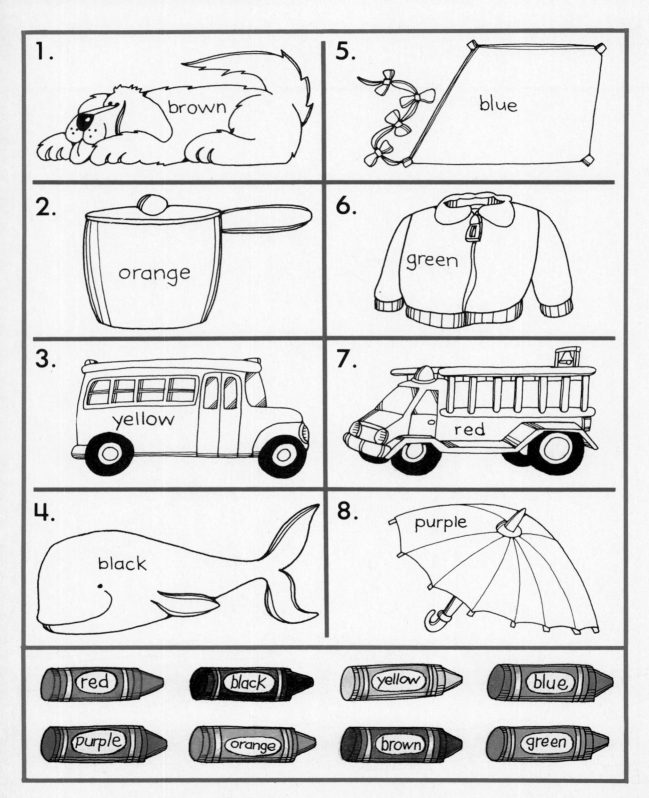

1. brown

2. orange

3. yellow

4. black

5. blue

6. green

7. red

8. purple

red   black   yellow   blue

purple   orange   brown   green

Children color pictures according to teacher's directions.

LISTENING

3 | up, down, in, out

 Listen and color.

Children listen to directions and color people and objects that are up, down, in, and out.

Readiness: Listening and Thinking

LISTENING

4 | Top, Middle, Bottom

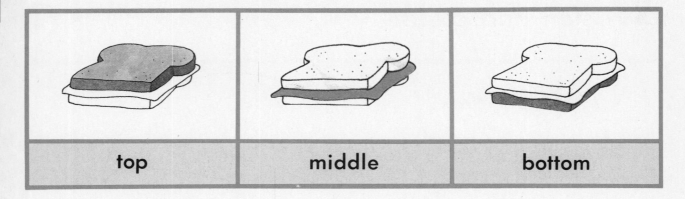

| top | middle | bottom |

Listen and color.

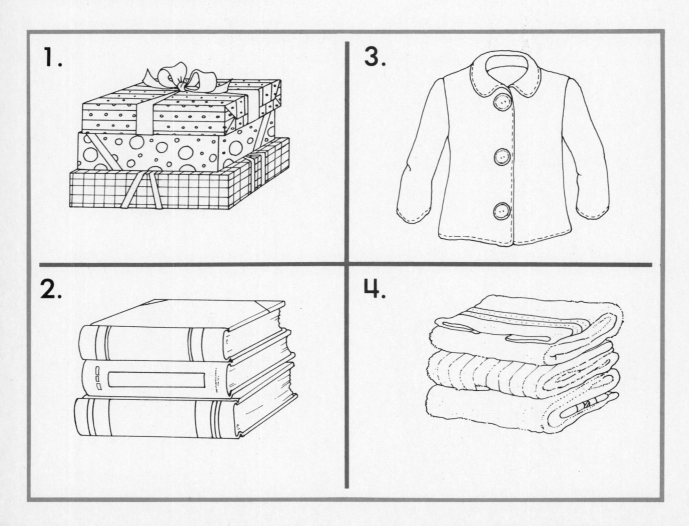

1.

2.

3.

4.

Children listen to directions and color objects in the top, middle, or bottom position.

Name

LISTENING

5 | Left and Right

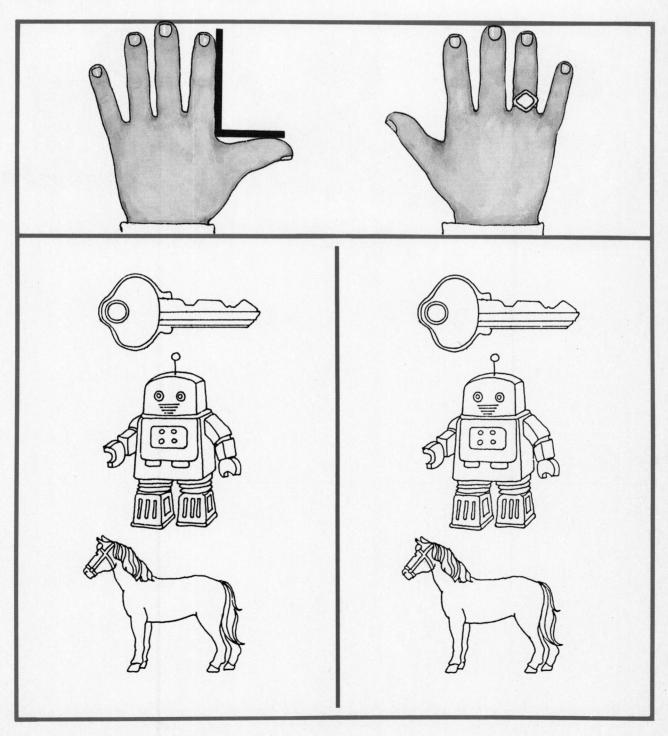 Listen and color.

Children listen to directions and color objects on their left-hand and right-hand sides.

Readiness: Listening and Thinking   37

THINKING

6 | First, Next, Last

 Talk about the pictures.

first	next	last
first	next	last

Readiness: Listening and Thinking

Children discuss order words. Then they cut pictures from page 39 and paste them in correct sequence here.

First, Next, Last continued

 Cut and paste.

Children cut out these pictures and paste them in correct sequence on page 38.

Readiness: Listening and Thinking

Name _____

THINKING

7 **Which Is Different?**

 Look and mark.

Children mark the object in each row that is different.

Readiness: Listening and Thinking 41

Name _____

8 | Matching Shapes

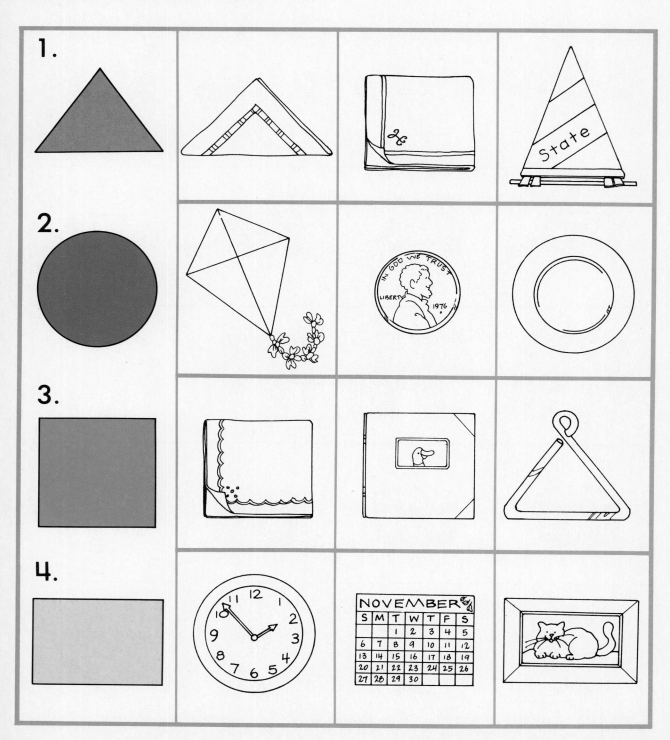 Look and color.

Readiness: Listening and Thinking

Children color objects in each row that match the shape at the beginning of the row.

THINKING

9 | Grouping Objects

Look and match.

1.
2.
3.
4.

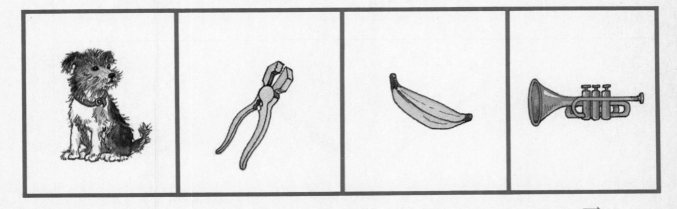

Children group objects by category.

Readiness: Listening and Thinking

Grouping Objects continued

 Look and mark.

Readiness: Listening and Thinking

Children group objects by function.

THINKING

10 | Signs

 Listen and mark.

Children follow directions to mark the correct signs.

Readiness: Listening and Thinking

Readiness
My Book of Favorites

1 | My Favorite Toy

Children draw and discuss pictures of their
favorite toys.

Name

2 | My Favorite Food

Readiness: My Book of Favorites

Children draw and discuss pictures of their favorite foods.

3 | My Favorite Animal

Children draw and discuss pictures of their favorite animals.

Name

4 | My Favorite Place

Readiness: My Book of Favorites

Children draw and discuss pictures of their favorite places.

5 My Favorite Storybook Character

Children draw and discuss pictures of their favorite
storybook characters.

6 | What I Like to Do Best

Readiness: My Book of Favorites

Children draw and discuss pictures of what they like to do.

7 | Making My Book

Children make books of their finished drawings,
using the covers provided at the back of the book.
They share their finished work.

Readiness: My Book of Favorites 53

Readiness
Letters and Numbers

1 | Tracing and Writing Letters

Look	Trace	Write

✏️ Trace and write each letter.

c c ☐ a a ☐ o o ☐

e e ☐ s s ☐

i i ☐ r r ☐

n n ☐ m m ☐

u u ☐ v v ☐ w w ☐

Children trace and write lower-case letters.

Readiness: Letters and Numbers

Tracing and Writing Letters continued

Look   Trace   Write

✏️ Trace and write each letter.

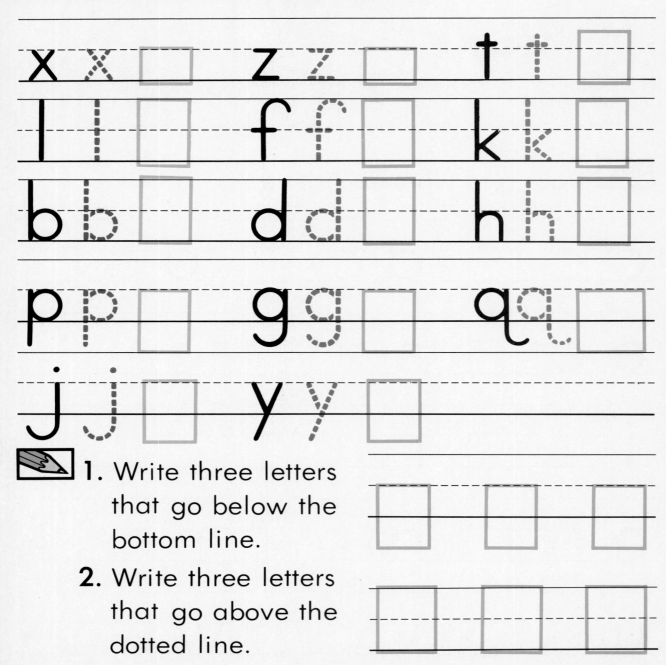

✏️ **1.** Write three letters that go below the bottom line.

2. Write three letters that go above the dotted line.

Children trace and write lower-case letters.

2 | Picture Clues

Name each picture. Trace and write the letter that begins each picture name.

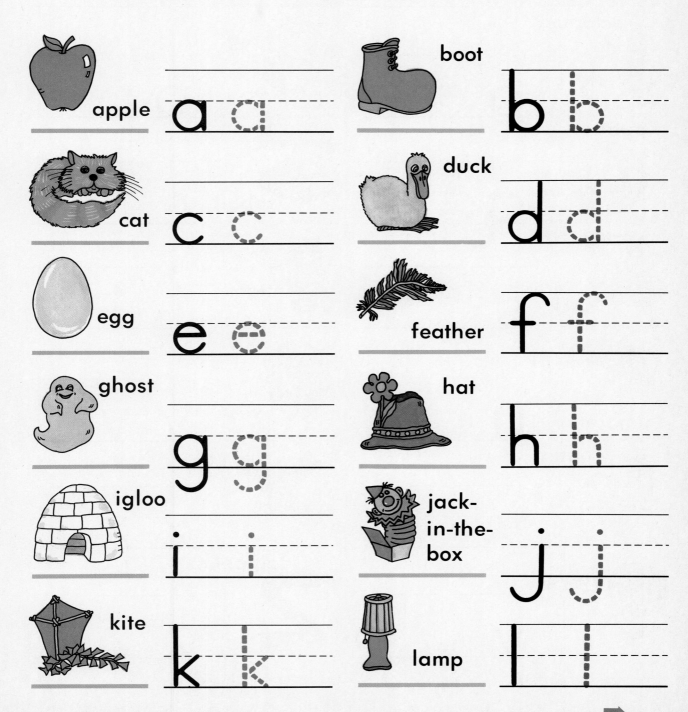

apple   a a

boot   b b

cat   c c

duck   d d

egg   e e

feather   f f

ghost   g g

hat   h h

igloo   i i

jack-in-the-box   j j

kite   k k

lamp   l l

Children trace and write lower-case letters.

Readiness: Letters and Numbers   57

Picture Clues continued

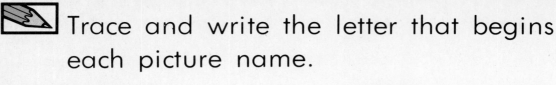

Trace and write the letter that begins each picture name.

monster — m

nest — n n

octopus — o o

pig — p p

quarter — q q

rabbit — r r

sock — s s

tiger — t t

umbrella — u u

vest — v v

worm — w

x x

yo-yo — y y

zipper — z z

Children trace and write lower-case letters.

3 | Writing Capital Letters in ABC Order

 Trace and write each letter.
The letters are in ABC order.

Children trace and write capital letters.

Readiness: Letters and Numbers

Writing Capital Letters in ABC Order continued

Trace and write each letter.

M   M   M   N   N   N

O   O   O   P   P   P

Q   Q   Q   R   R   R

S   S   S   T   T   T

U   U   U   V   V   V

W   W   W   X   X   X

Y   Y   Y   Z   Z   Z

Children trace and write capital letters.

4 | Tracing and Writing My ABC's

 Trace and write the letters.
The letters are in ABC order.

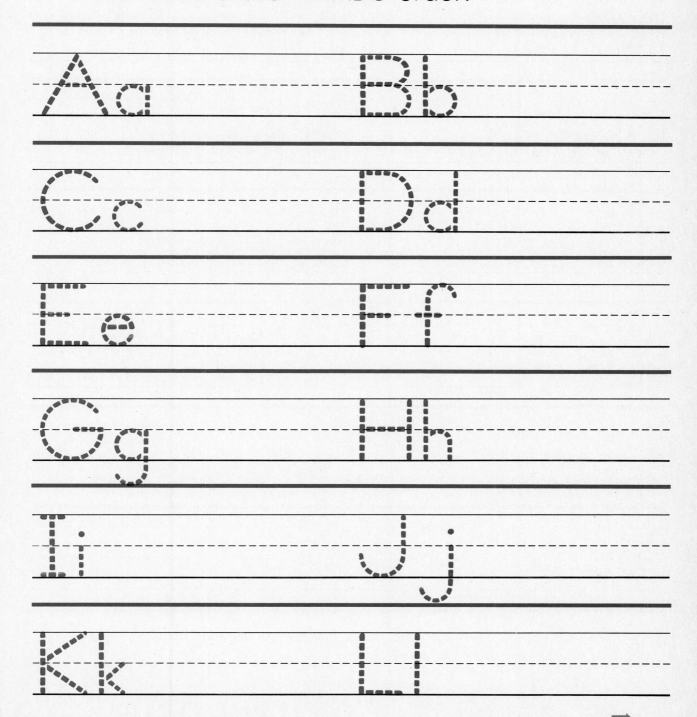

Children trace and write capital and
lower-case letters.

Tracing and Writing My ABC's continued

Trace and write the letters.

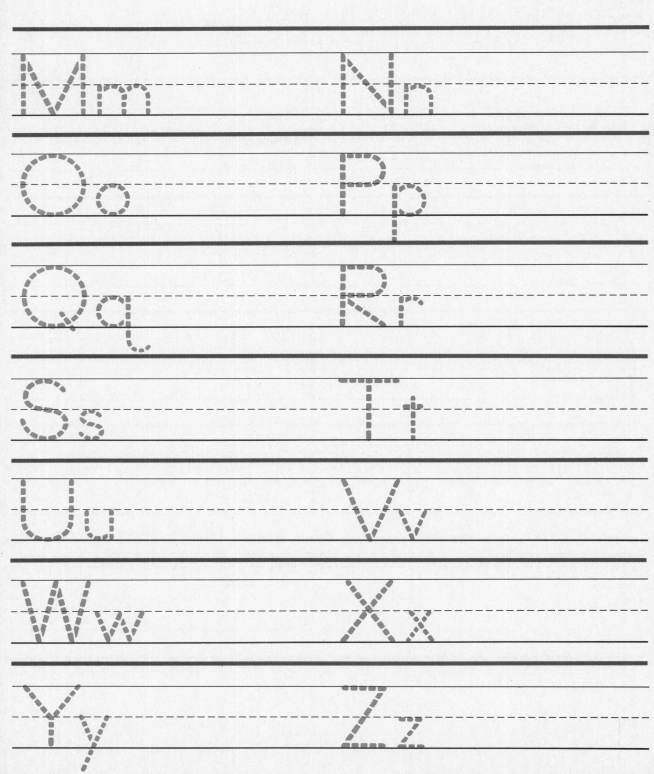

Readiness: Letters and Numbers

Children trace and write capital and lower-case letters.

5 | ABC Order

These letters are in ABC order.
Write the missing letters.

A B C ☐ E F ☐

H I J ☐ L M ☐

O P Q R S T ☐

V W X ☐ Z

---

a b ☐ d e f ☐ h i

j ☐ l m n o ☐ q

r ☐ t u v ☐ x y z

Children write letters in ABC order.

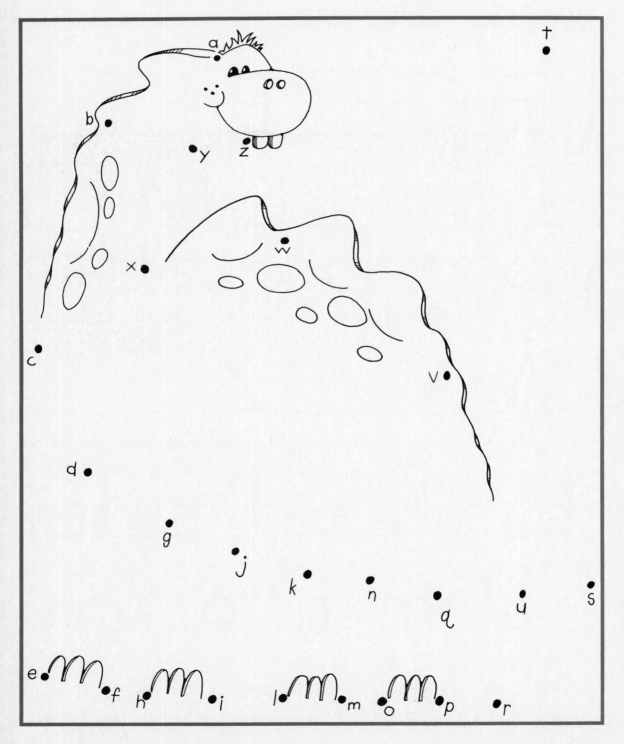

Draw a line from letter to letter.
Use ABC order. Color your picture.

Readiness: Letters and Numbers

Children connect the dots in ABC order.

6 | Tracing and Writing Numbers

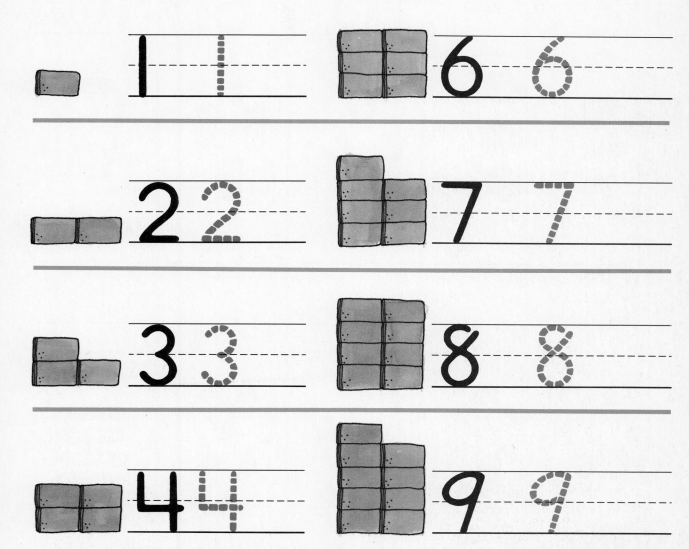

Trace and write the numbers.

1   1 1

6   6 6

2   2 2

7   7 7

3   3 3

8   8 8

4   4 4

9   9 9

5   5 5

10   10 10

Children trace and write numerals.

Readiness: Letters and Numbers

Tracing and Writing Numbers continued

Trace the numbers. Then count the objects and write the correct number.

1 2 3 4 5 6 7 8 9 10

8

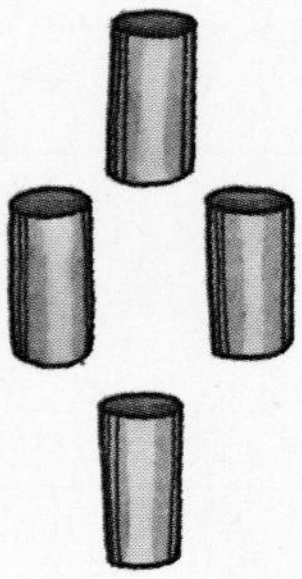

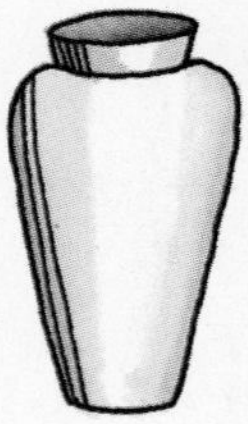

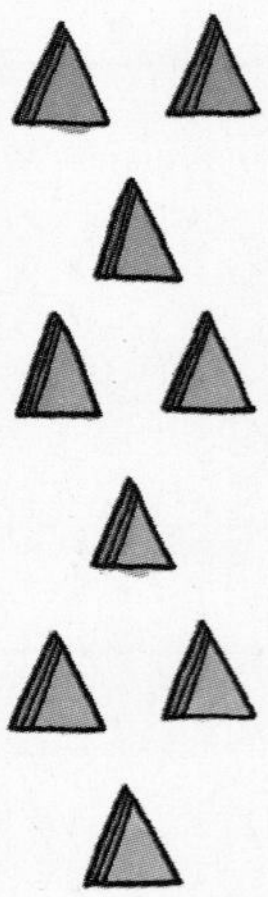

Readiness: Letters and Numbers

Children count objects and trace and write numerals.

Name _____

7 | Number Words

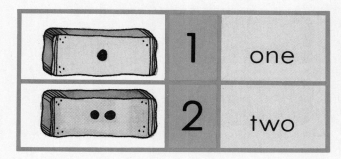

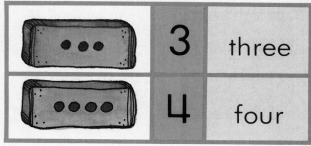

✏️ Trace each number word.
Draw pictures to show the number.

1
one ___one___

3
three ___three___

2
two ___two___

4
four ___four___

Children trace number words and draw an
equivalent number of objects.

Readiness: Letters and Numbers ➡ **67**

Number Words continued

🟫	**5**	five
🟫	**6**	six
🟫	**7**	seven

🟫	**8**	eight
🟫	**9**	nine
🟫	**10**	ten

✏️ Trace each number word.
Draw pictures to show the number.

5
five

8
eight

6
six

9
nine

7
seven

10
ten

Children trace number words and draw an
equivalent number of objects.

8 | Phone Numbers I Need

 Write the names and phone numbers.

My number: _____

Parent's work:

Name _____

Number _____

Neighbor:

Name _____

Number _____

Children write important phone numbers.

Readiness: Letters and Numbers

Grammar
Sentences

Name

1 | Speaking in Sentences

 Look at the picture. Tell about it.

Children use sentences to describe picture.

Grammar: Sentences

Name

2 | Naming Parts

Every sentence has two parts.
The **naming part** names someone or something.

✏️ Trace the naming parts.

1. <u>This story</u> tells about a fox.

2. <u>A rabbit</u> comes to his house.

3. <u>The friends</u> eat lunch.

✏️ Match the sentence parts.

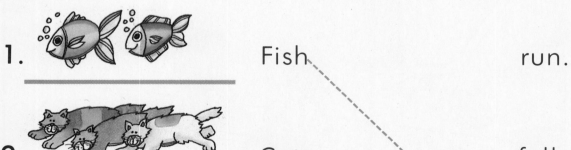

1.   Fish   run.

2.   Cats   fell.

3.   The pencil   swim.

Children trace and match naming parts (subjects).

Name

3 | Writing Naming Parts

Every sentence has a **naming part.**

 Write a naming part for each sentence.

A duck	**The rabbit**	**Mother**	**Tom**	**Kim**

1. Kim _____ hits the ball.

2. _____ swims in a lake.

3. _____ eats a plant.

4. _____ paints a picture.

5. _____ pats the dog.

Children write naming parts (subjects).　　　　　**Grammar: Sentences**　**73**

Name _____

Every sentence has two parts.
The **action part** tells what someone or
something does.

 Trace the action parts.

1. Bob  fell down.

2. He lost his pencil.

3. Three boys helped him.

 Match the sentence parts.

1. This bell   walks to school.

2. My cat   rings loudly.

3. Fred   sleeps all day.

Children trace and match action parts (predicates).

Name _____

Every sentence has an **action part**.

 Write an action part for each sentence.

| paints | | laughs | |
| reads | | fly | |

1. Ducks _____fly_____.

2. Dad _____.

3. My sister _____.

4. Joey _____.

6 Matching Sentence Parts

Naming Parts	Action Parts

Match naming parts and action parts.
Write the sentences.

1. My friend laughs.

2.

3.

Children write sentences.

7 | Finding Sentence Parts

Every sentence has two parts.

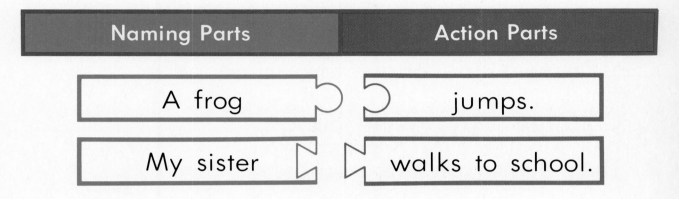

| Naming Parts | Action Parts |

A frog ⊃ ⊂ jumps.

My sister ⊐ ⊏ walks to school.

✏️ Circle the naming parts.

1. (The cat) plays on the rug.

2. The cat plays with a ball.

3. Tabby hits the ball.

4. The ball rolls away.

5. This cat likes to play.

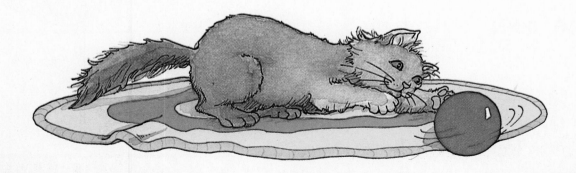

Children identify naming parts (subjects).

Grammar: Sentences

Finding Sentence Parts continued

Naming Part	Action Part
My cat	sleeps.

✏️ Draw a line under the action parts.

1. Children <u>play in the park.</u>

2. They swing on the swings.

3. The girls run to the lake.

4. The boys make boats.

✏️ Draw a line between the naming parts and the action parts.

1. The boy | plays.

2. The cow eats hay.

3. Sue digs a hole.

Children identify naming parts (subjects) and action parts (predicates).

Name _____

8 | Which Is a Sentence?

Naming Part	Action Part
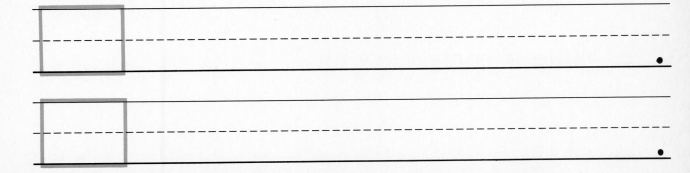	
Karen	threw the ball.

 Read these word groups.
Write the two sentences.

1. the rabbit

2. The rabbit ran.

3. jumped up

4. She jumped up.

[ ] _____

[ ] _____ •

[ ] _____

[ ] _____ •

Children identify sentences.

9 | Writing **I** in Sentences

Always write the word **I** as a capital letter.

John and **I** read books.

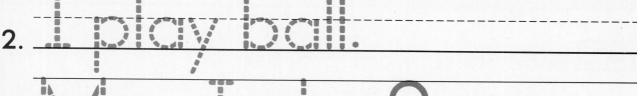Trace these sentences with **I**.

1. I can run.

2. I play ball.

3. May I play?

4. Will I win?

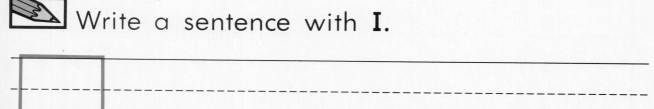Write a sentence with **I**.

Grammar: Sentences

Children write the word **I** in sentences.

Name

Building Vocabulary

Opposites are words like **stop** and **go**.
The words **hot** and **cold** are also opposites.

 Write the word that belongs in each sentence.

1. A rabbit is fast.

A turtle is  slow.

 fast

 slow

2. The tree is big.

_____

The plant is _____ •

 big

 small

3. The boy walks up.

_____

The girl walks _____ •

 up

down

4. The cat is in.

_____

The dog is _____ •

 in

 out

Children write opposites.

Grammar: Sentences **81**

Grammar-Writing Connection
Writing Sentences

Write a sentence for each picture.

Naming Part + Action Part

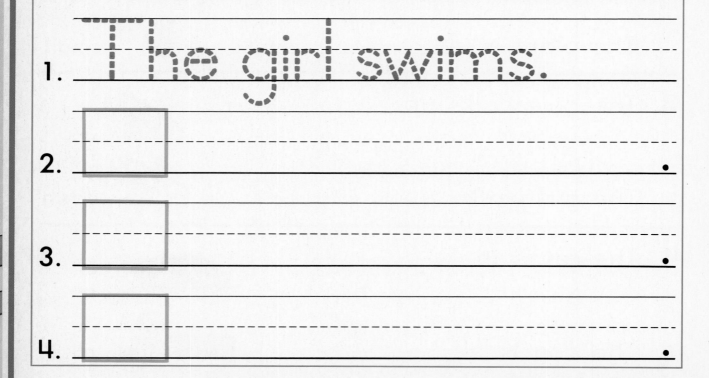

1. The girl swims.

2.

3.

4.

Children write sentences.

Name _____

Check Up: Unit 6

 Write a naming part for each sentence.

Bobby

The bell

1. _____ rings.

2. _____ plays ball.

 Write an action part for each sentence.

counts

sleeps

sails

1. The cat _____ .

2. The boy _____ .

3. The boat _____ .

 Write **I** to complete these sentences.

1. _____ found a key.   2. May _____ go?

Reading and Writing Class Story

LITERATURE
Lunch for a Dinosaur
By Bobbi Katz

I'm fixing a lunch for a dinosaur.
Who knows when one might come by?
I'm pulling up all the weeds I can find.
I'm piling them high as the sky.
I'm fixing a lunch for a dinosaur.
I hope he will stop by soon.
Maybe he'll just walk down my street
And have some lunch at noon.

Lost in the Museum

By Miriam Cohen

THE WRITING PROCESS

1 | Talking Together

 The children in this class talked about what they had done together. They made a list of story ideas.

What has your class done? Make a list. Choose one idea for a story.

Children generate topics for a class story and choose one.

Name _____

 Draw a picture of what your class did.

Tell about your picture.

Children draw and discuss pictures about the topic for the class story.

THE WRITING PROCESS

3 | Writing Our Story

This class wrote a story together.
Here is the story.

We made puppets. We used bags. We colored them. We had a show. Our parents came. They liked it.

Talk about your story.
Tell your teacher what you want to write.

Children discuss sample story and dictate a first draft to teacher.

Reading and Writing: Class Story

THE WRITING PROCESS

4 | Writing More

The class talked about the story.
Then they wrote more.

On the chart paper:

                    animal
We made ∧puppets. We used
paper   We drew faces on them.
∧bags. We colored them. ∧We had

a show. Our parents came. They

liked it.

Read your class story together.
What do you want to add?

Reading and Writing: Class Story

Children discuss sample class story and revise their class story.

THE WRITING PROCESS

5 | Making a Final Copy

This is the final copy of the class story.

OUR CLASS STORY

Our Puppet Show

We made animal puppets. We used paper bags. We colored them. We drew faces on them. We had a show. Our parents came. They liked it.

How can you show your class story?

Children discuss ways to display the final copy of their class story.

Reading and Writing: Class Story

Grammar
More About Sentences

1 ‖ Sentences Make Sense

A **sentence** makes sense. The words are in order.

me swims duck the to

(The duck swims to me.)

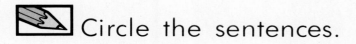 Circle the sentences.

The top is big.
is big top the

play to cats like
Cats like to play.

goes car the fast
The car goes fast.

A bird can fly.
can fly bird a

Children identify sentences.   **Grammar: More About Sentences**

2 | Sentences Tell

Sentences that tell are **telling sentences.**

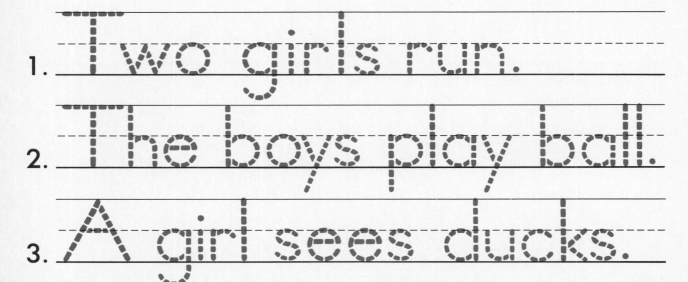

Trace these telling sentences.
They tell about the picture.

1. Two girls run.

2. The boys play ball.

3. A girl sees ducks.

Grammar: More About Sentences

Children trace telling sentences.

3 | Writing Capital Letters

A **telling sentence** begins with a **capital letter.**

This snake is long.

Begin each sentence with the word in the box.
Begin each sentence with a capital letter.

1. houses   Houses _____ have doors.

2. fish   _____ swim.

3. rabbits   _____ have tails.

4. balls   _____ are round.

5. grass   _____ is green.

Children capitalize the first words of sentences.   **Grammar: More About Sentences** 95

Name

4 | Writing Periods

A **telling sentence** ends with a **period.**

This train is long.

Put a period in the ○ at the end of each sentence.

1. I like boats○

2. My friend likes boats○

3. Some boats are long○

4. My boat is red○

Copy each sentence. End it with a period.

1. I like cars

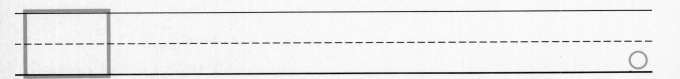
○

2. Jill likes boats

○

Grammar: More About Sentences

Children supply periods to end sentences.

5 | Sentences Ask

Sentences that ask are **asking sentences**.

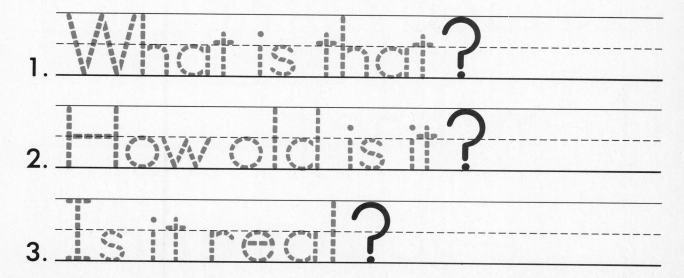

Trace these asking sentences.

1. What is that?

2. How old is it?

3. Is it real?

Children trace asking sentences (questions).   **Grammar: More About Sentences**   97

6 | Writing Question Marks

An **asking sentence** begins with a **capital letter**.
An **asking sentence** ends with a **question mark**.

Is your mother here**?**

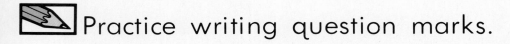Practice writing question marks.

? ? ?

Trace the capital letters.
Write the question marks.

1. Is Bob home

2. May I help

3. Are you asleep

Grammar: More About Sentences

Children write question marks and capital letters.

Name

Circle the question words in the picture.
Copy them.

_____   _____

_____   _____

_____   _____

_____

Children write question words.

Grammar: More About Sentences 99

Name _____

8 | Telling Sentences and Asking Sentences

Telling sentences end with **periods.**
Asking sentences end with **question marks.**

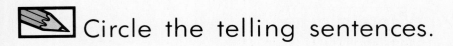 Circle the telling sentences.

1. Do you have any books?

2. (I have ten books.)

3. I like books very much.

4. My mother reads books too.

5. Do you like to read?

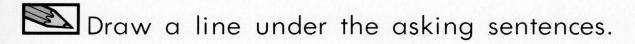 Draw a line under the asking sentences.

1. When is the party?
   _____

2. I don't know.

3. How old is Patty?

4. Where does she live?

5. What will you give her?

100   **Grammar: More About Sentences**

Children identify telling sentences and asking sentences.

Name _____

My Shadow
by ROBERT LOUIS STEVENSON

I have a little shadow
that goes in and out with me,
And what can be the use of him
is more than I can see.
He is very, very like me
from the heels up to the head;
And I see him jump before me,
when I jump into my bed.

 Trace **I** or **me.**

1.  have a little shadow.

2. He is very, very like

3.  see him jump before

Children trace **I** or **me.**

Grammar: More About Sentences   **101**

Name _____

Building Vocabulary

 Write the sound-alikes in each sentence.

bee   **B**

1. The _____ buzzes.

2. C comes after _____.

son   **sun**

3. Jay is his _____.

4. The _____ is hot.

ate   **eight**

5. Manuel _____ lunch.

6. Jo has _____ cats.

Grammar: More About Sentences

Children supply correct sound-alikes (homophones) in sentences.

Name _____

Grammar-Writing Connection
Writing Telling and Asking Sentences

Copy these telling and asking sentences. Begin and end them the right way.

1. how old are you

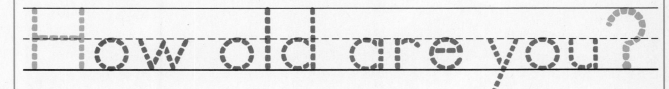

2. i am six

_____

- - - - - - - - - - - - - - - - -

_____

3. when is your birthday

_____

- - - - - - - - - - - - - - - - -

_____

- - - - - - - - - - - - - - - - -

_____

4. my birthday is May 7

_____

- - - - - - - - - - - - - - - - -

_____

✏ Write a telling sentence about the picture.

_____

- -

_____

- -

✏ Write an asking sentence about the picture.

_____

- -

_____

- -

Children write telling and asking sentences.

Check Up: Unit 8

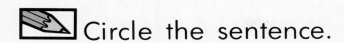 Circle the sentence.

1. milk likes cat the   2. The bear runs.

✎ Begin each sentence with a capital letter.

1. | a | _____ dog has a tail.

2. | tommy | _____ plays ball.

✎ End these sentences the right way.

1. Where do you live ____

2. I live at home ____

✎ Write **me** in these sentences.

1. Sal gave _____ a kite.

2. Please play with _____ .

Children review skills covered in Unit 8.   **Grammar: More About Sentences** **105**

Reading and Writing Letters

The Pickety Fence

By David McCord

The pickety fence
The pickety fence
Give it a lick it's
The pickety fence
Give it a lick it's
A clickety fence
Give it a lick it's
A lickety fence
Give it a lick
Give it a lick
Give it a lick
With a rickety stick
Pickety
Pickety
Pickety
Pick

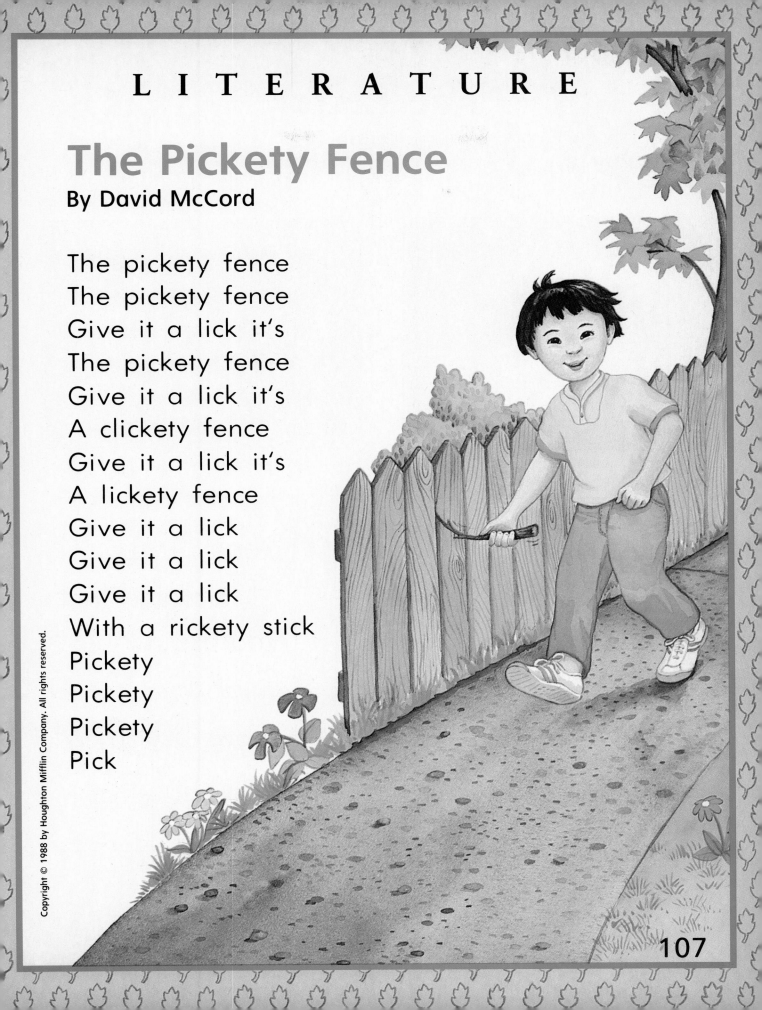

The Letter
By Arnold Lobel

Dear Toad,
   I am glad that
you are my best
friend.
   Your best friend,
      Frog

COMPOSITION SKILL

1 | Kinds of Letters

Look at these letters. What do they tell?

Dear Carol,
　　We are having fun.
I like the lake.
　　　　Your friend,
　　　　Alice

Dear **Ling**,
Please come to my
birthday party
Day: Sunday, August 7
Time: 2:00
Place: 10 Forest Street
Your friend,
Abigail

Dear Auntie,
Thank you for
my book. I can
read it.
　　Love,
　　Daniel

Children discuss three types of letters.

Reading and Writing: Letters 109

Name _____

Look at this invitation.

Dear <u>Brian</u> ,
Please come to my
<u>birthday party</u> .
Day: <u>Saturday, January 8</u>
Time: <u>1:00</u>
Place: <u>382 Reed Road</u>
     Your friend,
     Laura

Answer these questions.

1. Who will get it? _____

2. What day is the party? _____

3. What time? _____

4. Where? _____

Children discuss an invitation and write the answers to questions about it.

Name _____

3 | Writing an Invitation

 Fill in this invitation.

_____

- -

Dear _____ ,

Please come to

_____

- -

_____ •

_____

- -

Day: _____

_____

- -

Time: _____

_____

- -

Place: _____

_____

- -

_____

Children write invitations.

Reading and Writing: Letters

THE WRITING PROCESS

4 | I Can Write to . . .

Who would like a letter from you?
Draw pictures of two people.

Reading and Writing: Letters

Children draw pictures of people to whom they can write and choose one.

Name _____

5 | I Can Tell About . . .

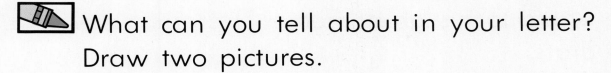 What can you tell about in your letter?
Draw two pictures.

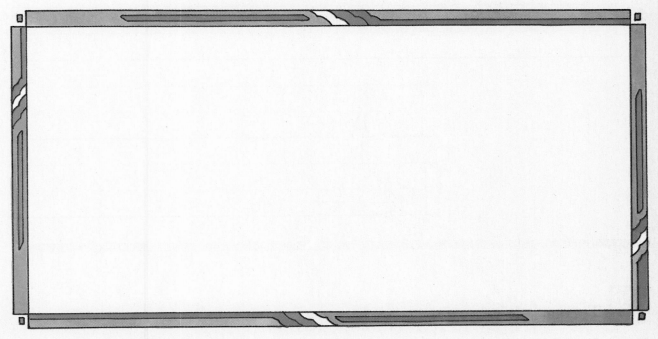

Children draw pictures of possible letter topics and
choose one.

Reading and Writing: Letters

THE WRITING PROCESS

6 | Pete's Letter

Pete wrote to his grandmother. Here is his first draft.

Dear Grandmother,
How are you. i
like kamp. We swim
We play.

Love,
Pete

Talk about Pete's letter.

Reading and Writing: Letters

Children discuss sample student letter.

Name _____

7 | Writing My Letter

Look at the pictures you drew in Lessons 4 and 5. Now write your letter.

Dear _____ ,

_____

_____

_____

_____

_____ ,

_____

8 | Writing More

Pete read his letter to a friend.
Then he wrote more.

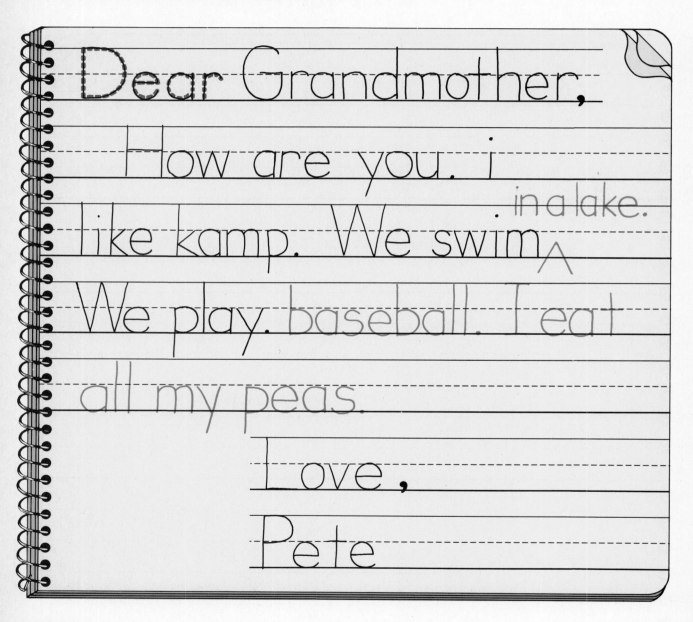

Dear Grandmother,

How are you. i

like kamp. We swim . in a lake.

We play. baseball. I eat

all my peas.

Love,

Pete

Read your letter to someone.
Talk about it. What can you add?

Children discuss the revised student sample and revise their own letters.

9 | Proofreading

Pete looked at his letter again.
He made these changes.

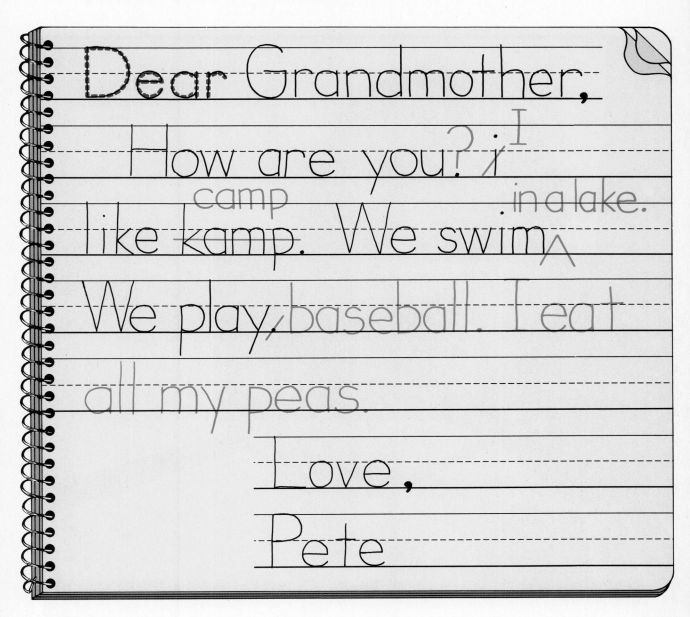

Dear Grandmother,

How are you? ; I
~~camp~~
like ~~kamp~~. We swim ^ in a lake.

We play, baseball. I eat

all my peas.

      Love,

      Pete

 Now check your letter.
What can you change?

Children discuss the proofread student sample and
proofread their own letters.

Reading and Writing: Letters

Name _____

10 Making a Final Copy

Pete wanted his letter to look neat.
He copied his letter onto another piece of paper.

 Copy your letter onto the next page.

Reading and Writing: Letters

Children make final copies of their letters.

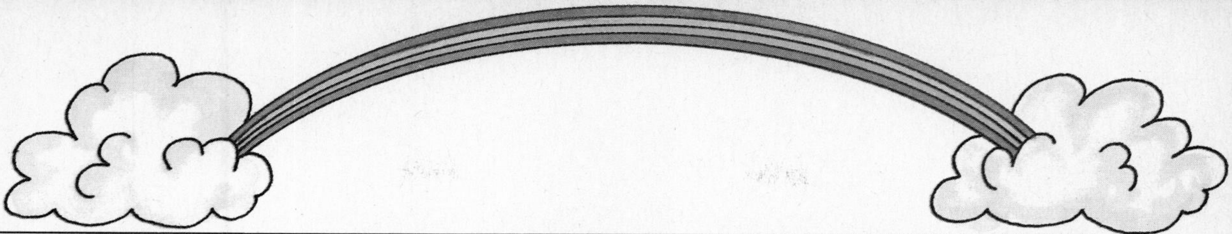

Dear _____ ,

_____

_____

_____

_____

_____

_____

_____

_____ ,

_____

THE WRITING PROCESS

11 | Mailing My Letter

Pete wanted to mail his letter.
Talk about what he did.

Pete Ward
25 Elm St.
Boston, MA 02108

A Nation of
Readers

Mrs. Ellen Beach
16 Overlook Road
Dallas, TX 75234

Children discuss mailing their letters.

Reading and Writing: Letters 121

Grammar
Naming Words

1 | Naming Words

Some words are **naming words**.

boy	hat	park
dog	frog	book

Write the naming words for these pictures.

1. dog

4. _____

2. _____

5. _____

3. _____

6. _____

Children write naming words (nouns).   **Grammar: Naming Words** 123

Name _____

2 | Naming Words for People

Some **naming words** name **people**.

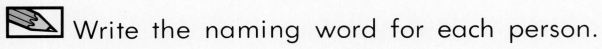 Write the naming word for each person.

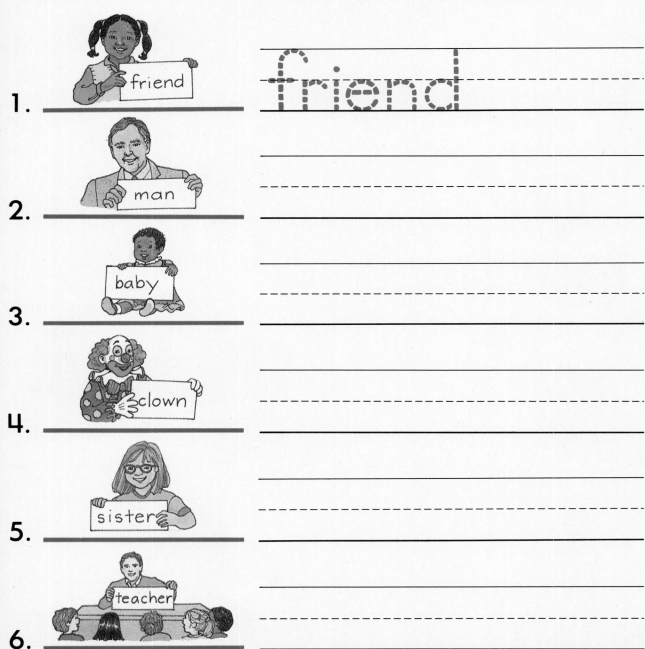

1. friend

2.

3.

4.

5.

6.

Grammar: Naming Words

Children write naming words (nouns) for people.

3 Naming Words for Animals

Some **naming words** name **animals**.

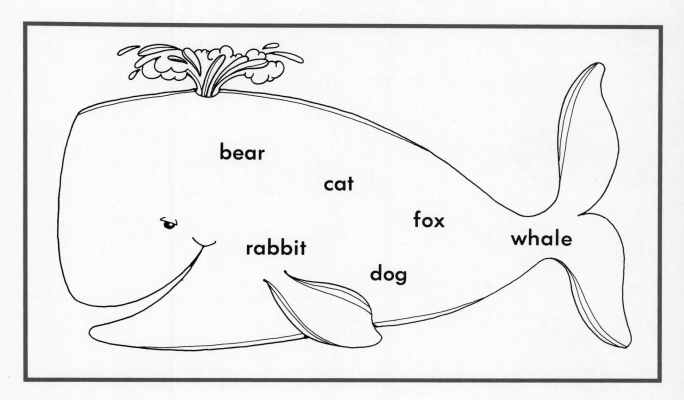

✏️ Copy the naming words for animals.

bear

Children write naming words (nouns) for animals.

Grammar: Naming Words

4 | Naming Words for Things

Some **naming words** name **things.**

Match the pictures and the words.
Write the naming word for each thing.

pencil 

car

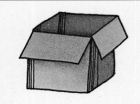

coat

boat

kite

box

    Children write naming words (nouns) for things.

5 | Naming Words for Places

Some **naming words** name **places**.

 Write the naming word for each place.

house house

pond

store

school

park

6 | Naming Words in Sentences

Naming words name **people, animals, things,** and **places.**

 Finish the sentences. Use naming words from the word box.

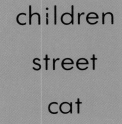
children

street

cat

1. My pet 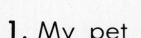 is black.

2. The _____ like school.

3. I like the houses on my _____ •

 Write a naming word for each sentence.

1.  The _____ is red.

2.  I saw the school _____ •

Children write naming words (nouns) in sentences.

7 One and More Than One

Some naming words mean one.

boat

Some naming words mean more than one.

boats

An **s** means more than one.

 Draw a picture for each word below.

books	trees	flowers
ball	keys	pen

Children distinguish between one (singular) and more than one (plural).

Grammar: Naming Words

One and More Than One continued

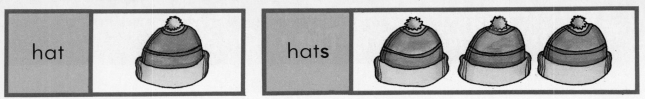

hat		hats	

✏️ Circle the words that mean more than one.
Then write them.

1. father (fathers) _fathers_

2. homes   home _____

3. rooms   room _____

4. wing   wings _____

5. roads   road _____

✏️ Write the words. An **s** means more than one.

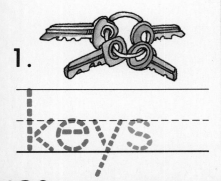

1. _keys_

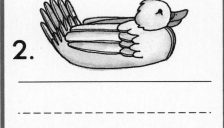

2. _____

3. _____

130   **Grammar: Naming Words**

Children distinguish between one (singular) and
more than one (plural).

8 | Special Names

People have **special names**. Carol Ben

Places have **special names**. Freed Park

Some **animals** have **special names**. Ruff

A **special name** begins with a **capital letter**.

 Write the special name the right way.

1. ron   Ron

3. Ann   ann

_____

2. fluffy   Fluffy

_____

4. denver   Denver

_____

Children write special names (proper nouns).

Grammar: Naming Words   **131**

A **special name** begins with a **capital letter.**

Jan

Reed **S**chool

Laddie

 Circle the special names.

(Sue)	New Park	Andy
boy	Ruff	dog
Juan	Ashton	Mr. Smith
cat	Clear Lake	Liz

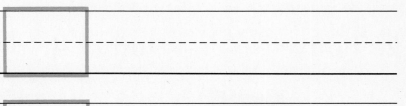 Write some special names.

1. your name

2. a friend

3. another friend

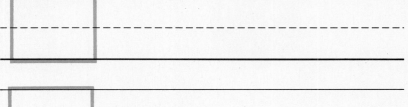

132   **Grammar: Naming Words**

Children identify and write special names (proper nouns).

9 | Days of the Week

The name of each day begins with a **capital letter**.

✏️ Write the name of each day.

Sunday   Sunday

Monday   ⬜

Tuesday   ⬜

Wednesday ⬜

Thursday ⬜

Friday   ⬜

Saturday ⬜

Children write and capitalize the days of the week.

Grammar: Naming Words

10 | Months of the Year

The name of each month begins with a **capital letter**.

January 	February	March	April
May	June	July	August
September	October	November	December

✏️ Write the month for each special day.

Halloween   October

Valentine's Day

Thanksgiving

   Children write and capitalize months of the year.

11 | Seasons of the Year

The seasons are **fall**, **winter**, **spring**, and **summer**.
The names of the seasons <u>do not</u> begin with capital letters.

fall

September
October
November

winter

December
January
February

spring

March
April
May

summer

June
July
August

 Finish these sentences.

1. Thanksgiving is in the 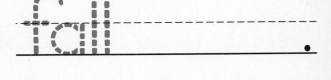 .

2. My favorite season is _____ .

3. My birthday is in the _____ .

Children write the seasons of the year.

Grammar: Naming Words

12 | <u>he</u>, <u>she</u>, <u>it</u>

He, she, and it can take the place of naming words.

 Trace **he**, **she**, and **it**.

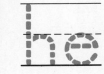 **h e**    **s h e**   **i t**

boy   girl   hat

 Draw a line to **he**, **she**, or **it**.

1.  - - - - - she

Linda   he

3.  he

bed   it

2. grandfather   he   it

4. kite   she   it

 Write **he**, **she**, or **it**.

1. **s h e**

sister

2. _____

brother

3. _____

ball

4. _____

girl

Children write **he**, **she**, **it** (pronouns).

Building Vocabulary

Some words are made from two words.

dog + house = doghouse

 Add two words to make a new word.
Write the new words.

1. door + bell =  doorbell

2. foot + ball = _____

3. star + fish = _____

 Draw pictures.

birdhouse   bookbag

Children write compound words.

Grammar: Naming Words

Grammar-Writing Connection
Writing Naming Words in Sentences

 Finish these sentences with special names.

1. My name is _____ .

2. I go to _____ School.

3. This month is _____ .

4. Monday comes after _____ .

 Write a sentence about this picture.

Children complete sentences with naming words (nouns) and write an original sentence.

Check Up: Unit 10

 Write the naming words for these pictures.

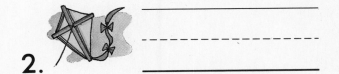

1. _____

2. _____

3. _____

4. _____

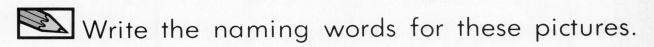 Write the words for the pictures.

1. _____

2. _____

Draw a line under the special names.

boy Jack	cat Fluffy	road East Road

Draw a line under the right word.

january	Wednesday	June	monday	Spring
January	wednesday	june	Monday	spring

Children review skills covered in Unit 10.

Grammar: Naming Words

LITERATURE

Move Over
By Lilian Moore

Big
burly
bumblebee
buzzing
through the grass,
move over.

Black and
yellow
clover rover,
let me pass.

Fat and
furry
rumblebee
loud on the
wing,
let me
hurry
past
your sting.

The Owl
By Jack Prelutsky

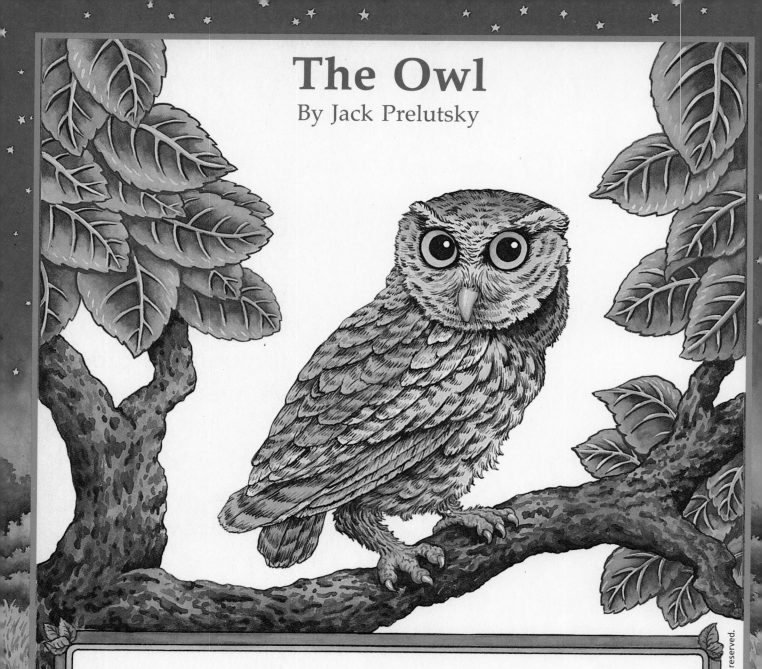

The owl is wary, the owl is wise.
He knows all the names of the stars
    in the skies.
He hoots and he toots and he lives
    by his wits,
but mostly he sits . . . and he sits . . . and
    he sits.

The Lion and the Mouse

from Aesop retold by Marie Gaudette

One day, Lion came down from
a tree. It had been a long hot day.
Lion was hungry. But he was
too tired to hunt for his supper.
"I will rest now," said Lion.
"When it is dark, I will hunt."
Lion lay down in the tall
yellow grass. He went to sleep.
Lion had pale yellow hair. It
looked just like the grass. It
fooled a little mouse. The mouse
ran right up on Lion's back.

 Listen to the rest of the story.

Name _____

1 | Beginning, Middle, End

 Talk about the pictures.

Draw what happens.

Children discuss the beginning and the middle of a story and provide an ending for it.

Reading and Writing: Story

145

Name _____

2 | Story Ideas

✏️ Draw two ideas for a story.

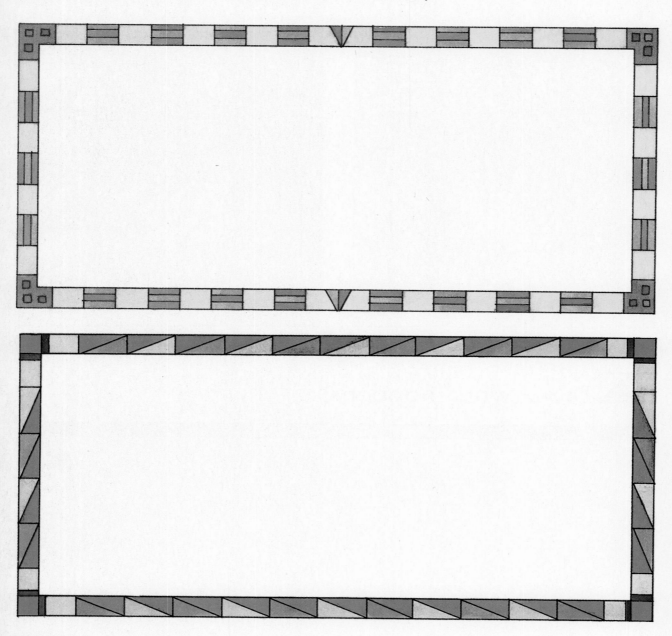

Talk about your pictures with someone.
Choose one for a story.

Children draw pictures of possible story topics and choose one.

Name

 Draw what will happen at the beginning of your story.

Draw what will happen at the end.

Now tell your story to someone.

Children use their drawings to tell their own stories.

Reading and Writing: Story

Name _____

4 | Jan's Story

Jan wrote a story. Here is her first draft.

I found a box? Joe found a ball. There ws a magic key. i opened the box.

 Talk about Jan's story.

Children discuss the first draft of a sample story.

Name _____

5 | Writing My Story

Look back at the pictures you drew in
Lesson 3. Write your story.

Children write a first draft of the story they
told in Lesson 3.

Reading and Writing: Story

6 | Writing More

Jan read her story to Kevin.
Then she made changes.

I found a box? ~~Joe~~
                    magic
                    ^
~~found a ball.~~ There ws
a magic key. i opened
the box. It was filled
with toys.

Read your story to someone.
Talk about it.
What can you add?
What can you change?

Children discuss the revised student sample and revise their own stories.

Name

Jan looked at her story one more time.
She made these changes.

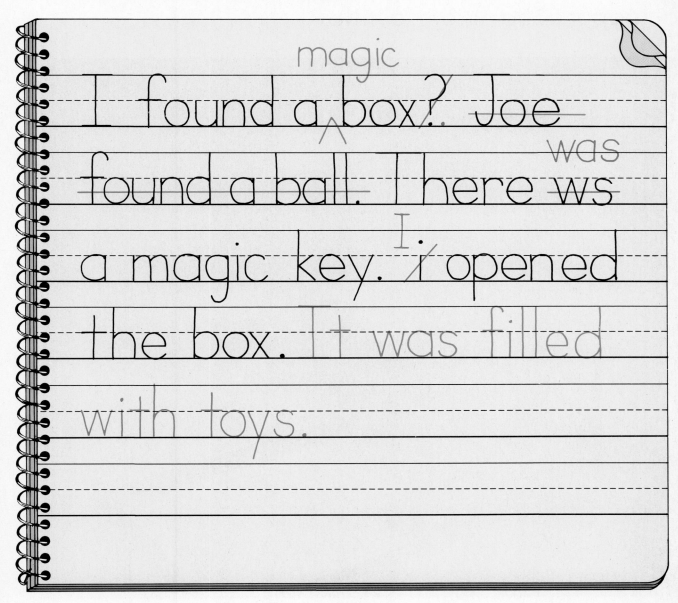

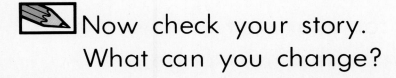 Now check your story.
What can you change?

Children discuss the proofread student sample and
proofread their own stories.

Reading and Writing: Story 151

THE WRITING PROCESS

8 | Making a Final Copy

Jan wanted her story to look neat.
She copied her story onto another piece
of paper. She wrote a title.

Think of a title for your story.
Write your story on the next page.

Children add a title and copy their final drafts.

THE WRITING PROCESS

9 | Making My Book

Jan made her story into a book.

Make your story into a book.
Use the covers in the back of this book.

Children make books of their finished stories and share them in class.

Reading and Writing: Story

Name

1 | Action Words

Some **action words** tell
what people and
animals do.

The boys **sing.**

Trace the action word for each picture.

1. run

4. talk

2. hop

5. laugh

3. read

6. jump

Children trace action words (verbs).

Grammar: Action Words 157

Action Words continued

Some **action words** tell
what people and
animals do.

The ducks **walk.**

Match the pictures and the words.
Write each action word.

play   play

eat

jump

fly

run

sing

158   **Grammar: Action Words**

Children write action words (verbs).

Name _____

USAGE

2 | Action Words with One and More

Some action words tell about more than one.

The bells ring.

Some girls jump.

Some action words tell about one.
Action words that tell about one end in **s**.

The bell ring**s**.

A girl jump**s**.

✏️ Trace the action words.

1. This dog ⌇runs⌇.

2. The boys ⌇talk⌇.

3. My little sister ⌇sits⌇.

Children trace action words (verbs) that
agree in number with subjects of sentences.

Grammar: Action Words 159

Action Words with One and More continued

This cat sits.

Three cats sit.

✏️ Write the correct action word.

1. A dog **barks** •
barks
bark

2. The dogs _____ •
barks
bark

3. The boy _____ •
sings
sing

4. Six boys _____ •
sings
sing

Children write action words (verbs) that agree in number with subjects of sentences.

Name _____

Use **is** in a sentence about one.
Use **are** in a sentence about more than one.

This boy **is** happy.

These boys **are** happy.

 Trace **is** and **are**.

1. This girl ___is___ six.

2. The bird ___is___ small.

3. These girls ___are___ friends.

4. Many birds ___are___ here.

5. This duck ___is___ big.

Children trace **is** and **are** in sentences.

Grammar: Action Words

is and are continued

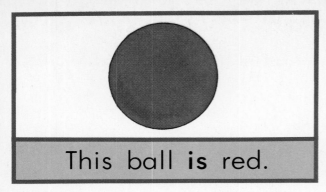 This ball **is** red.

 These balls **are** red.

 Write **is** or **are** to finish each sentence.

1. The tables _____ long.
   is   are

2. His car _____ green.
   is   are

3. This box _____ big.
   is   are

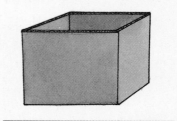

4. Some cats _____ brown.
   is   are

5. This baby _____ happy.
   is   are

Children write **is** and **are** in sentences.

Name _____

4 | Adding <u>ed</u>

Add **ed** to some action words to tell about the past.

Now	Past
I play now. I jump today.	I play**ed** last night. I jump**ed** yesterday.

 Trace the action words.

1. We _painted_ before lunch.

2. We _rest_ now.

3. Today I _call_ Grandfather.

4. Yesterday Grandmother _called._

5. Last night we _walked_ home.

Children trace action words (verbs) in the present and past tenses.

Grammar: Action Words

Adding **ed** continued

Add **ed** to some action words to tell what happened in the past.

 Draw a line under the action words that tell about the past.

<u>quacked</u>	work
ask	walked
talked	looked
showed	walk
play	rolled
laughed	played

 Write these words in the sentences.

counted   jumped   cooked

1. The cat _____ into the boat.

2. We _____ the money.

3. Dad _____ breakfast.

Children choose and write action words (verbs) in the past tense.

5 | Action Words in Sentences

Some action words tell what people and animals do.

 Complete each sentence with an action word from the box.

| works | swims | eat | sleeps | help |

1. My dog <u>sleeps</u> in a bed.

2. The men _____ lunch.

3. I _____ my father.

4. A bear _____ in the lake.

5. Mr. Long _____ at the school.

Children complete sentences with action words (verbs).

Grammar: Action Words

Action Words in Sentences continued

Look at the pictures.
Write an action word for each sentence.

1. The little rabbit _____ .

2. Sue and Bill _____ wood.

3. Mrs. James _____ the cars.

Children complete sentences with action words (verbs).

Name _____

Use **was** in a sentence about one.
Use **were** in a sentence about more
than one.

This dog **was** in.

These dogs **were** out.

 Trace **was** and **were**.

1. Jan ___was___ sick.

2. Ann and Rosa ___were___ asleep.

3. Father ___was___ at home.

4. Mom and I ___were___ in the kitchen.

was and **were** continued

Bob **was** hot.

Jill and Jim **were** cold.

 Draw a line under the correct word.

1. The girls (was <u>were</u>) lost.

2. Sue (was were) sad.

3. Juanita (was were) scared.

4. Soon the girls (was were) back.

5. Mother and Father (was were) happy.

 Write **was** or **were**.

1. Two ducks _____ here.

2. One cup _____ on the table.

Children write **was** and **were** correctly in sentences.

7 | isn't, don't, can't

Isn't means **is not**.
Don't means **do not**.
Can't means **cannot**.

This mark **,** takes the place of missing letters.

✏️ Match the words that mean the same.

is not ----------------- don't

cannot -----------------isn't

do not   can't

✏️ Trace each word.

1.

2.

3.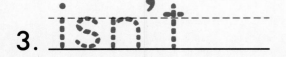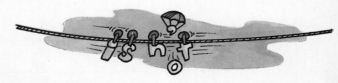

Children match and trace **isn't**, **don't**, and **can't** (contractions).

Grammar: Action Words

isn't, don't, can't continued

✏️ Trace **isn't**, **don't**, and **can't**.

1. Mary *isn't* my sister.

2. They *don't* live there.

3. Bud *can't* swim.

✏️ Write **don't**, **isn't**, or **can't**.

1. I do not see Bob.

   _____

   I _____ see Bob.

2. He is not here.

   _____

   He _____ here.

3. We cannot find him.

   _____

   We _____ find him.

170   **Grammar: Action Words**

Children trace and write **isn't**, **don't**, and **can't** (contractions) in sentences.

Name _____

Building Vocabulary

 Write the better action word.

1. He  in the parade.
marched   walked

2. Ted _____ under the table.
goes   crawls

3. Paula _____ the milk.
pours   spills

4. The kitten _____ up.
jumps   gets

Children choose and write the more precise action word (verb) in each sentence.

Grammar: Action Words   **171**

Grammar-Writing Connection
Writing Action Words in Sentences

Look at the picture. Write two sentences about what the people are doing.

1. _____

_____

_____ •

2. _____

_____

_____ •

Children write sentences.

Check Up: Unit 12

 Write the correct action word.

```
                    _____
                    - - - - - - - - - - - - - - - -     sing
1. The girl _____•     sings


                    _____
                    - - - - - - - - - - - - - - -     eat
2. Three cats _____•     eats


               _____
               - - - - - - - - - - -                is
3. Matt _____ tall.     are


                    _____
                    - - - - - - - - - - - - - - -      is
4. Matt and Bob _____ tall.     are
```

Draw a line under the action words that tell about the past.

1. walked   4. talked

2. jump   5. helped

3. laughed   6. call

1 | Looking and Describing

Look at the pictures.
Trace the words that describe what you see.

flowers

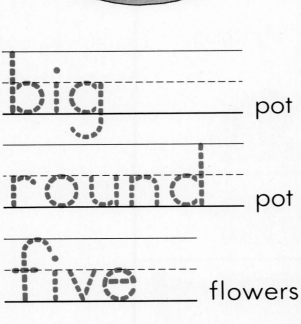

pot

flowers

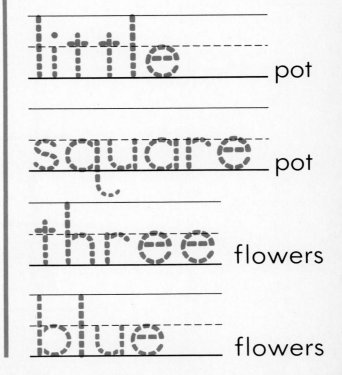

pot

big _____ pot

round _____ pot

five _____ flowers

red _____ flowers

little _____ pot

square _____ pot

three _____ flowers

blue _____ flowers

Children trace describing words (adjectives).

Grammar: Describing Words 175

Name _____

 Trace the words that describe taste, smell, and sound.

1. The pickle tastes sour.

2. This flower smells sweet.

3. The drum sounds loud.

 Match the words and pictures.

salty

sour

soft

loud

176   **Grammar: Describing Words**

Children trace and match describing words (adjectives).

3 | Describing How Things Feel

How would each thing feel?
Write a word from the box.

soft	cold	wet
hard	hot	dry

soft

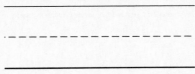

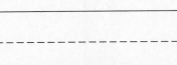

Children write describing words (adjectives).

Grammar: Describing Words

4 | Using Describing Words

Look at the word box. Write the words that describe each picture.

wet shoe	long bat	red rug
dry shoe	short bat	blue rug

short bat

Children write descriptions of pictures.

Name _____

5 │ Describing Words in Sentences

Describing words tell how things look, taste, smell, sound, and feel.

 Use describing words from the box. Finish the sentences.

| fresh | sweet | loud | hot | square |

1. The country air smells  fresh.

2. A pear tastes _____ .

3. The window is  _____ .

4. The toy made a  _____ sound.

5. The _____ soup is here.

Children complete sentences, using describing words (adjectives).

Grammar: Describing Words **179**

Name _____

6 | Choosing the Better Description

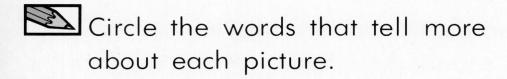 Circle the words that tell more about each picture.

   a toy

(a brown teddy bear)

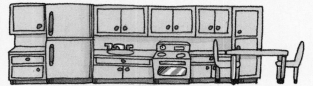   a long yellow kitchen

a room

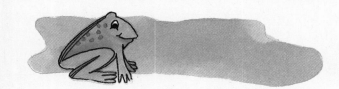   an animal

a little green frog

✏️ Write the word from each box that describes the picture.

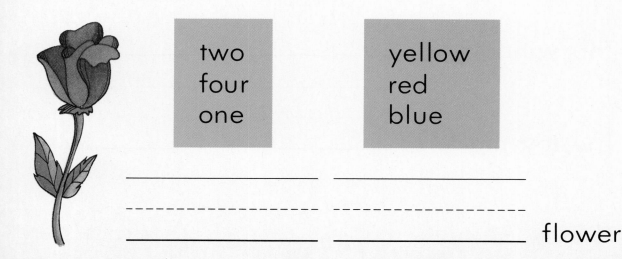

| two four one | yellow red blue |

_____ _____

_____ _____

_____ _____ flower

180   **Grammar: Describing Words**

Children choose the better of two descriptions.

Name _____

Look at the brushes. How are they different?

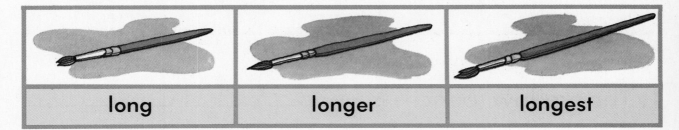

| long | longer | longest |

 Add **er** and **est** to the first word.
Write the new words.

tall   <u>taller</u>   <u>tallest</u>

  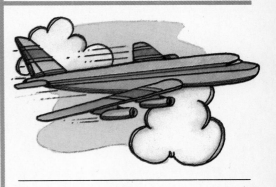

fast   _____   _____

Children write comparative and superlative forms
of adjectives.

Grammar: Describing Words   **181**

Adding <u>er</u> and <u>est</u> continued

 Finish the sentences.

| short | shorter | shortest |

1. The yellow pencil is  short.

2. The green pencil is _____ .

3. The red pencil is _____ .

| large | larger | largest |

1. The brown house is _____ .

2. The blue house is _____ .

3. The red house is _____ .

Grammar: Describing Words

Children complete sentences with comparative and superlative forms of adjectives.

Building Vocabulary

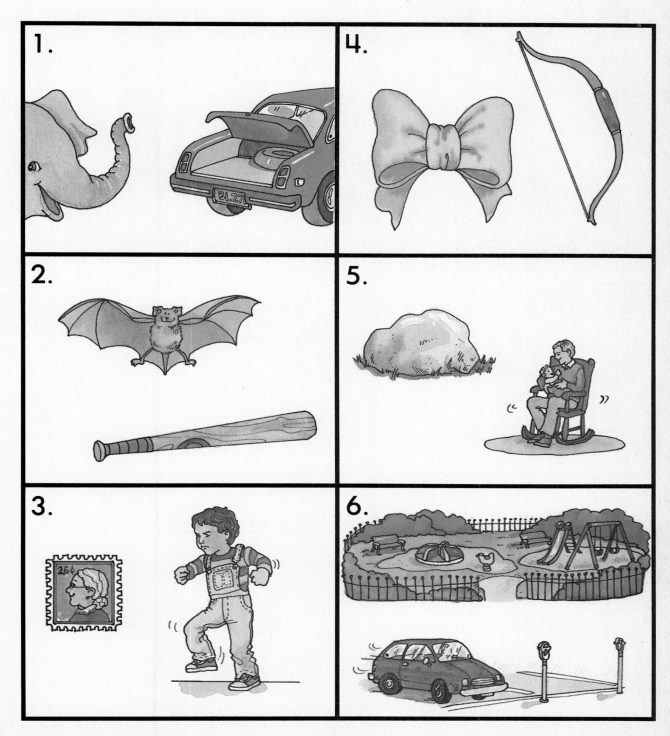

Listen. Draw a line under the right picture.

1.

2.

3.

4.

5.

6.

Children listen and underline the picture that
illustrates the correct homograph.

Grammar: Describing Words

Grammar-Writing Connection
Writing Describing Words in Sentences

Write two sentences that tell about the picture. Use describing words.

1.

2.

Grammar: Describing Words

Children generate and write descriptive sentences.

Check Up: Unit 13

 Circle three words that describe the rabbits.

red   soft   sour   one   two   brown

 Circle two words that describe ice.

soft   hard   green   cold

 Draw lines to match the words and the pictures.

small

smaller

smallest

Children review skills covered in Unit 13.

Grammar: Describing Words   185

Reading and Writing
A Book Report

1 | The Library

A **library** is a place where many books are kept. You may borrow these books and take them home.

Write a sentence about what you would see or do in a library.

Children discuss and write about the resources in a library.

Reading and Writing: A Book Report

Name _____

2 | Thinking About a Book

Listen to a book.
The **title** is The Forgetful Bears.
The **author** is Lawrence Weinberg.

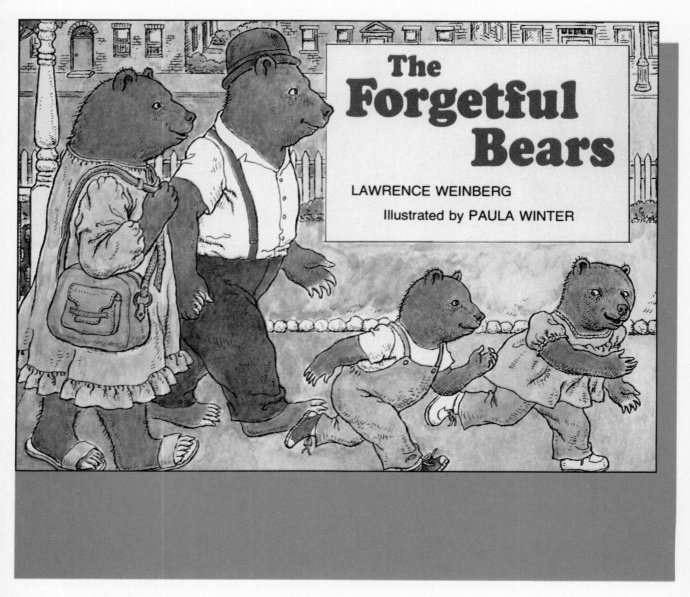

The
Forgetful
Bears

LAWRENCE WEINBERG

Illustrated by PAULA WINTER

Tell what you liked about the book.

188

Reading and Writing: A Book Report

Children listen to a book and discuss what they
liked about it.

3 | Sharing a Book

Kim wrote a book report.
Talk about what she wrote.

Title: <u>The Forgetful Bears</u>

Author: <u>Lawrence Weinberg</u>

This book is about <u>bears.</u>

<u>They forget</u>

<u>everything.</u>

I like this book because <u>it is</u>

<u>very funny.</u>

Children discuss a sample student book report.

Reading and Writing: A Book Report

Name

4 | A Book I Like

Write the title.

_____

- -

_____

Draw a picture of something that happens
in the book.

Reading and Writing: A Book Report

Children write titles of books they like and draw
pictures of what happens in those books.

Name

5 My Book Report

Write about your book.

Title:

Author:

This book is about

I like this book because

Children write simple book reports.

Student's Resource Book

Study Skills Lessons
1 Words in ABC Order

a b c d e f g h i j k l m n o p q r s t u v w x y z

dog　　**h**at　　**n**ame　　**t**ree

The words **dog, hat, name,** and **tree** are in **ABC order.**

Look at the words in each picture frame. Circle the first letter of each word. If the three words are in ABC order, color the frame red.

Children identify words in alphabetical order.

2 Words in a Dictionary

a b c d e f g h i j k l m n o p q r s t u v w x y z

A **dictionary** is a book about words. The words or pictures in a dictionary are in ABC order.

Circle the word that comes first in a dictionary.

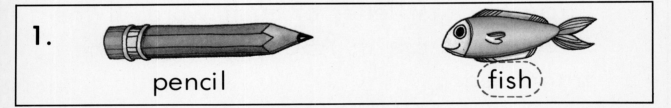

1. pencil   (fish)

2. hat   coat

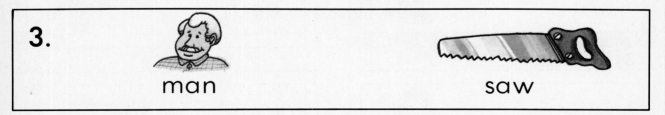

3. man   saw

4. turtle   rabbit

Children decide which word appears first in a dictionary.

3 Using a Dictionary

Words that begin with the same letter are in the same part of a dictionary. The words **<u>c</u>hildren**, **<u>c</u>oat**, and **<u>c</u>ow** are in the **C** part.

Circle the words you would find in the **B** part of a dictionary.

(boat)   cat   bat   box

book   girl   bird   bed

In which part of a dictionary would you find each word? Write the letter.

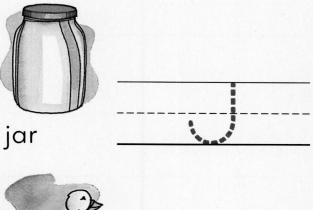

jar _____ J _____

key _____

duck _____

boat _____

Children determine where in a dictionary they would look for certain words.

4 Using My Picture Dictionary

Find each picture in your Picture Dictionary. Write the word for each picture.

1. apple

2.

3.

4.

5.

STUDY SKILLS LESSONS

Children find and write words from the Picture Dictionary, pp. 198–206.

5 Finding More Words

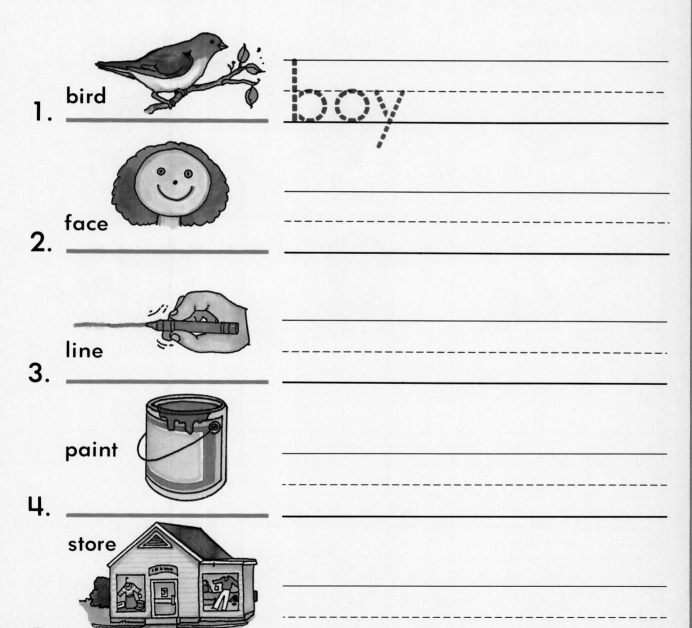 Find each word in your Picture Dictionary. Write another word that you find under the same letter.

1. bird — boy

2. face —

3. line —

4. paint —

5. store —

Children find and write additional words from the Picture Dictionary, pp. 198–206.

Picture Dictionary

Aa	Bb	Cc
animals	bird	children
apple	book	coat
arm	boy	cow

Student's Resource Book: Picture Dictionary

Children use the Picture Dictionary for spelling help and for dictionary lessons. Throughout the year, they add their own words on the lines provided.

Dd	Ee	Ff
dinosaur	ear	face
door	eat	father
duck	eye	foot

Children use the Picture Dictionary for spelling help and for dictionary lessons. Throughout the year, they add their own words on the lines provided.

Student's Resource Book: Picture Dictionary

Gg	Hh	Ii
game	hand	ice
girl	hot	ink
glass	house	iron

200 **Student's Resource Book: Picture Dictionary**

Children use the Picture Dictionary for spelling help and for dictionary lessons. Throughout the year, they add their own words on the lines provided.

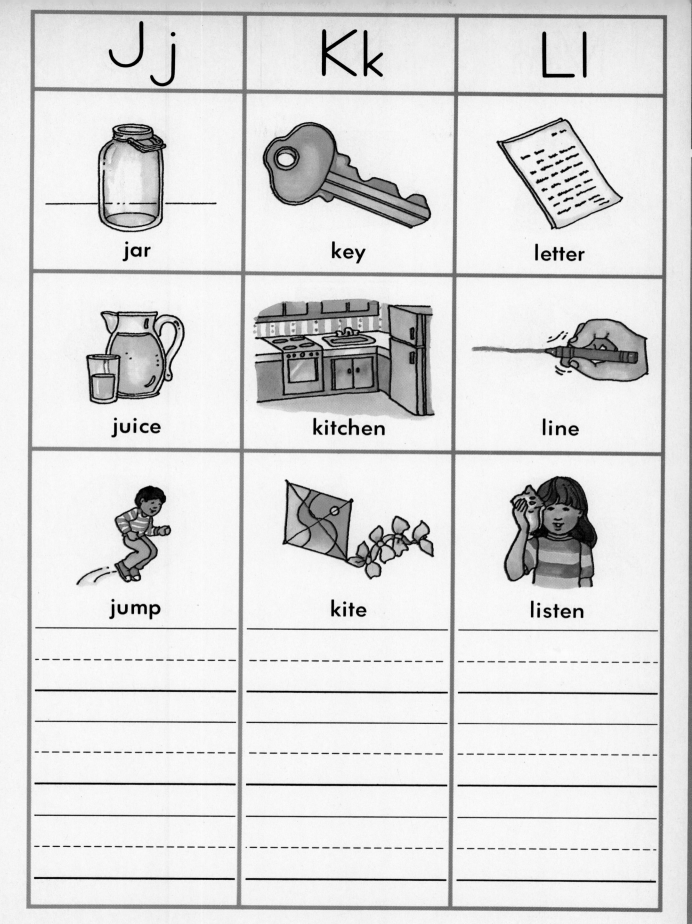

J j	K k	L l
jar	key	letter
juice	kitchen	line
jump	kite	listen

Children use the Picture Dictionary for spelling help and for dictionary lessons. Throughout the year, they add their own words on the lines provided.

Mm	Nn	Oo
man	new	one
moon	night	open
mother	note	orange

202 **Student's Resource Book: Picture Dictionary**

Children use the Picture Dictionary for spelling help and for dictionary lessons. Throughout the year, they add their own words on the lines provided.

Pp	**Qq**	**Rr**
paint	quarter	rain
people	queen	road
picture	quilt	rock

Children use the Picture Dictionary for spelling help and for dictionary lessons. Throughout the year, they add their own words on the lines provided.

Student's Resource Book: Picture Dictionary 203

Ss	**Tt**	**Uu**
school	table	umbrella
store	teacher	under
street	two	up

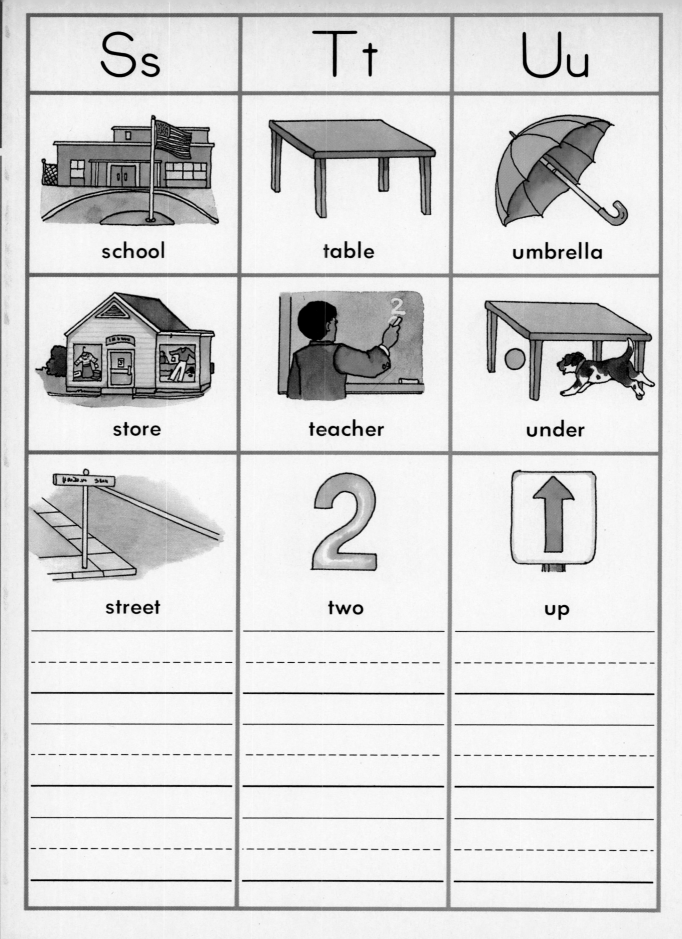

Student's Resource Book: Picture Dictionary

Children use the Picture Dictionary for spelling help and for dictionary lessons. Throughout the year, they add their own words on the lines provided.

Vv	Ww	Xx
van	walk	x-ray
vegetables	window	xylophone
violin	woman	

Children use the Picture Dictionary for spelling help and for dictionary lessons. Throughout the year, they add their own words on the lines provided.

Student's Resource Book: Picture Dictionary

Yy

yard

year

yo-yo

Zz

zebra

zipper

zoo

January February March April May June July August September October November December

A B C D E F G H I J K L M N O P Q R S T U V W X Y Z

206 **Student's Resource Book: Picture Dictionary**

Children use the Picture Dictionary for spelling help and for dictionary lessons. Throughout the year, they add their own words on the lines provided.

Index

Numbers in **bold type** indicate pages where skills are taught. Names in italics refer to the punchouts at the back of the pupil book.

INDEX